SCREEN TIME SANITY

LUMOS PRESS

Screen Time Sanity
The Crazy Easy Guide to Doing Technology With Your Kids

Copyright © 2018 | Kira Lewis and Michelle Myers

LUMOS PRESS

Publishing and Design Services:
MartinPublishingServices.com

ISBN: 978-0-9998421-0-2 (print), 978-0-9998421-1-9 (epub)

SCREEN TIME SANITY

THE
CRAZY EASY GUIDE
TO DOING TECHNOLOGY
WITH YOUR KIDS

KIRA LEWIS AND MICHELLE MYERS

LUMOS PRESS

Contents

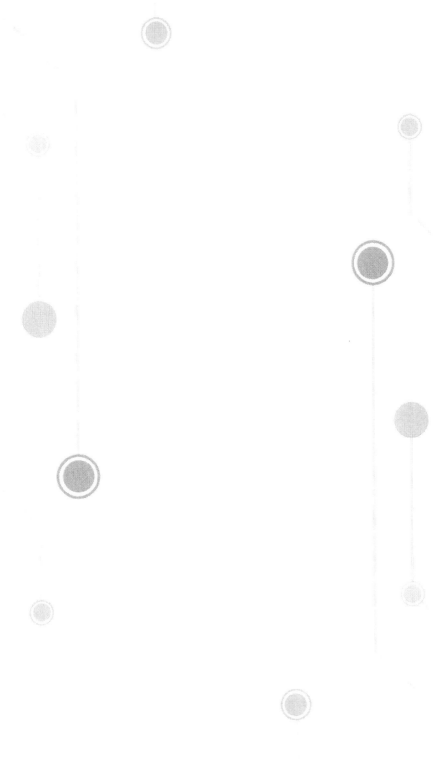

Technology 101 for Parents
– It Can Be Your "Thing"

We've all been there. Kids throwing tantrums because we made them turn off the tablet or told them it was time to stop playing Minecraft. Feeling like a failure, because we allowed too many hours of screen-time, but we hear so many conflicting stories we're not even sure how much screen time is okay at what age. Stress, because we're never sure if our kids might stumble onto inappropriate content.

Next come the battles over whether certain shows are too mature for them to watch. The constant whining about how they are the only one without a cell phone or a popular app. Pleas to be allowed social media accounts.

And then, no matter what ages are children are, we've all heard these stories. Children committing suicide after being bullied online, entire high schools being caught up in sexting scandals, children being seduced and even murdered by online predators. It's enough to bring fear into the heart of any parent.

These struggles and fears are only made worse by the total overwhelm that many parents feel about today's technology. The constant change and increasing complexity leave parents unsure about how to best parent and protect their children.

This is why Michelle and I began a parenting and technology series on our blog Sunshine and Hurricanes. We write all about smart parenting with purpose – and in today's world, being a smart parent means being smart about technology.

But we'll be honest; we weren't always so "smart" about this topic. Between us, we have six kids and we've been there, done that when it comes to just about every technology trouble you can imagine from toddler to teen.

We've dealt with the meltdowns when we've said "turn it off." We've struggled through trying to keep tech away from family mealtimes and out of kids rooms. We've faced the dilemma of how and to what extent we should be monitoring our kids tech use. Oh, and we totally know all about the guilt.

Guilt for allowing the kids to have way too much screen time because we needed to fix a meal, or finish a phone conversation, or simply because we didn't want to fight one more battle. Guilt for not watching them closely enough and having them stumble on something not meant for young eyes. Guilt because we didn't set rules from the beginning and now don't know how to get things back on track. We've felt your pain and we get it!

But we have not only felt your pain as parents, but as bloggers. Our work means we spend an enormous amount of time online, using social media and following parenting issues. On a daily basis, we observe the impact of technology on today's families and the stress it creates for parents. Often in response, we hear frustrated parents declare, *"Tech is just not my thing."*

Is that totally understandable? Of course it is. Technology can be really challenging for our society as a whole, not just for parents. But, here's the hard truth that you may not want to hear:

> If you're raising kids today,
> you really don't have a choice.
>
> TECH NEEDS TO BECOME
> YOUR "THING"!

It is not unusual for many parents to feel like technology – everything from tablets to mobile phones to YouTube and social media – is foreign, scary, and maybe even dangerous. Unlike our children, we were not all born with it as an everyday part of our lives. So, it isn't always intuitive to us and it can take time (precious time we often feel we don't have) to learn about and keep up with technology.

It is unfortunate that an overwhelming number of magazine articles, news clips, blog posts, and Facebook status updates focus so strongly on the negatives of technology and only reinforce a parent's fears and guilt. This endless stream of negative feedback keeps parents from seeing all the positive ways technology can be used for both fun and education when it comes to their children.

Even more concerning though, is the way it distracts parents from acknowledging that technology is an unavoidable part of their children's lives. It isn't going to go away.

Yes, it can be tempting to want to close our eyes and stick our fingers in our ears, hoping that it's all just one big fad. But avoiding it leaves you as a parent completely unequipped to guide your children and to keep them safe.

As Parents Today, Here's What We **DON'T** Want:

- We don't want our kids zoned out in front of the TV all day.

- We don't want them always choosing to play video games indoors when they can go outside and play.

- We don't want them failing to develop social skills like behaving in a restaurant because we were always handing over a device for their entertainment.

- We don't want our family relationships breaking down because everyone is too busy with their devices to talk to each other.

As Parents Today, Here is What We **DO** Want:

- We want to be involved in our children's educations and be able to help them.

  - ¿ Can we do that if we don't have some familiarity with one of the primary tools that they use?

- We want to do everything we can to keep our children safe.

  - ¿ Are we really doing everything, though, if we don't fully understand the true risks technology and social media pose to our children and how to guide them in their use?

- We want to raise children who are responsible, respectful, and compassionate.

  - ¿ Do we risk those character traits if we aren't able to explain and model the proper use and etiquette of technological devices and social media?

- *We want to encourage our children to pursue their dreams and become successful adults.*

  - ¿ Are we putting them at a disadvantage if we are unable to help them identify and use all the resources technology provides to help them pursue their passions and interests?

- *We want to strengthen our families and have fun with our children.*

  - ¿ Could we be losing an opportunity to bond with our children and to actually build our relationships if we refuse to learn and engage with them on a platform that is both fun and a BIG part of their life experience?

These questions aren't meant to be critical, but instead thought provoking.

They should challenge some of our pre-conceived notions or generational biases and maybe even help us reframe the issue.

Let's not forget there was a generation of parents way back when who thought rock and roll was simply noise and a fad that would soon pass – how'd that work out for them?

Getting up to speed with today's technology so you can be a more effective parent doesn't have to be painful. In this book, some basics are identified that will enable you to navigate today's technology with increased confidence, alleviate some of your worries, and empower you to be better guides for your children.

We cover all age groups. So, this is one of those books that you won't necessarily read from start to finish. Of course you can if you want to. But consider it a guide and a tool. If you've got little ones, it can help you get started on the right foot with how you handle technology in your household and keep you on track as they get older.

If you've got bigger kids, then use this book to help you tackle the tougher issues and the awkward topics that you might be shying away from. Let it empower you to put tech back in its place and put you back in control of your family.

Overall, it should be a resource that you can turn to whenever you're dealing with the parenting issues technology presents. Yes, it's true that in the years to come, technology will constantly evolve. But many of the parenting techniques we will be talking about are timeless.

Each generation of parents is presented with new and different challenges. But we're confident that by combining proven parenting principles with the strategies presented in this book, you'll be able to overcome these challenges and create some screen-time sanity in your home.

Setting Household Technology Rules

"I can't get my kids to stop playing on their DS/Wii/ PlayStation/iPad/Phone!"

"Anytime I tell them to turn it off, it turns into a major battle!"

"It feels like technology is taking over our lives!"

If you feel this way, you are NOT alone. Managing today's technology with kids can feel overwhelming for parents, but we really do have the ability to take control of technology before technology takes control of our families.

Step 1

There is an obvious starting place for this conversation – it's us parents. Before we can even begin to help our children to make wise choices when it comes to technology use, we have to ask ourselves: **exactly what behaviors are we modeling?** If we aren't exercising discipline and we're constantly on our devices, we can't expect anything different from our children.

"What you do speaks so loudly that I cannot hear what you say."

~Ralph Waldo Emerson

Step 2

We need some basic rules and boundaries that we've actually discussed with our kids and that we are sure they understand. So, here are some "house tech rules" that should help tame the technology monster that has taken over your household.

(A printable version of these rules is available on the resources webpage for this book, provided at the end of the book.)

1. Technology is a Privilege, Not a Right

As parents, we are obligated to provide some basics to our children. These are their rights as our children and include things like food, shelter, clothes, a K-12 education, and our love. Nowhere in the parent agreement does it state we MUST provide them with a TV, an iPhone, an iPad, a computer, two different gaming systems with games for each, and endless hours utilizing these various technologies. Those are NOT rights.

It's good to set boundaries with children. The reality is that their expectation for technology should be "zero," because as we've now stated, it is not anything we are obligated to give them to be considered good parents. As you convey this sentiment to them, you could bring your hands together to form a zero, kind of like you might if you were doing that cute little heart sign kids love to make these days.

Setting that line in the sand helps kids understand that having technology available and being given the opportunity to use it, beyond what might be required for their schooling, is not an automatic; they have to hold up their end of being part of the family, or technology is the first thing to go. It also helps them to be appreciative of technology time when they have it.

2. All Technology Must Be Parent-Approved

Whether it's watching a certain television show, downloading a new app, using the family computer, or purchasing a new video game, children MUST ask permission. If they do not, and this includes at other people's houses, the consequence should be a loss of all technology.

Each family has to determine for themselves the length of the time-out from tech based on the offense, but for this to be effective a zero-tolerance policy without exceptions is best. If you are unsure about whether or not something is appropriate for your child, a simple visit to a site like Common Sense Media (commonsensemedia.org) will provide you with all the info you need.

3. We Value People More Than Technology

How often has your child completely ignored a request you've made because they are zombified by the TV? Or maybe you've heard your children using unkind words when they are playing a video game with a friend or sibling? Our children need to learn to value their relationships, and that those relationships should always be put first.

If your child fails to respond to you, because they are too absorbed in technology, then turning the technology off for the rest of the day – and sometimes the rest of the week – is not unreasonable.

When it comes to how your child treats people when technology is involved, whether it's smack talk gone too far when playing video games (probably for older kids) or the use of texting or social media to be cruel to another child, removing their access to the technology is the most logical consequence.

However, it is also important to talk with them about why they made the choices they did and how to make better choices next time. If the behavior persists, then don't be afraid to have your child "take a break" for a determined amount of time until they can prove they are deserving of another opportunity.

4. Devices Don't Come to the Dinner Table

Period. End of story. (And yes, this applies to adults too). This is the best chance we have as parents to connect with our children and find out what is going on in their lives. If everyone is too busy with tech, then we lose out on this important family time.

5. There is No Tech Behind Closed Doors

There is plenty of evidence showing that it is not a great idea for children to have TVs, computers, and other technology in their bedrooms. However, this is really a family-by-family choice. Whatever you choose though, there is NEVER a reason that a child (toddler to teen) needs to have technology of any kind behind a closed door. It simply invites trouble, and while most of us want to trust our kids, why provide temptation that isn't absolutely necessary?

Parenting Tech Tip for 4 and 5: Many parents have said that having a basket where everyone, including Mom and Dad, puts their devices during meals and at bedtime can be an easy way to keep tech from intruding on family time and restful sleep. You may get a little pushback at first, but once the habit is formed, it usually becomes a non-issue.

6. Chores and Homework Come Before TV and Video Games

This goes back to technology being a privilege and not a right. Our kids need to be able to put their responsibilities to their family first and to adopt the "work before play" principle. This is also a step in teaching our children about priorities and how to put first things first.

7. Turn it Off is NOT a Negotiation

Demanding that our children turn off the TV or quit an electronic game they are playing without some sort warning isn't fair to them. The better approach is to give a five-minute notice before they are expected to turn it off. After the grace period is up, though, you can set the expectation that they are not to beg for more time, whine and complain, or even worse, have some sort of tantrum. In the event one of these outcomes occurs, again remove their technology privileges for a set period. When they get tech time back, remind them why they lost it and that they will have the consequence doubled if it happens again.

8. You Break it, You Help Pay to Replace It

Let's face it: Most technology is expensive. It is okay to talk with our kids about the investment made in a purchase and the importance of caring for possessions properly. For our littles, we need to show them the right and wrong way to handle these different devices; for all our kids, there should be an established safe place to put things when they are done using them.

If our kids are careless, then they absolutely need to, at a minimum, share the burden of paying for a replacement. For older kids, this money can come out of an allowance or savings, or they can do extra chores to earn the money to help replace the broken item. Younger children may not be able to monetarily help, but sharing the burden may mean an item just isn't replaced – or if it is, they no longer can use it.

9. Use Technology Appropriately or Lose It

Using tech in a way that could potentially harm any human being, including oneself, is inappropriate. This means having age-appropriate conversations with our children about the dangers that exist online. There needs to be a clear understanding about the language and photos that are acceptable vs. unacceptable to be posted online. Plus, we should never assume our child "knows better" – we must be blunt and state the obvious.

We also need to coach children on appropriate social etiquette and how to be respectful online. Children, and many adults, feel a false sense of anonymity when they are interacting with others online and may act in ways or say things that they never would in other situations.

We can have good kids, but that doesn't mean they will ALWAYS make good decisions. Children do not have fully developed decision-making capabilities or the ability to think through their decisions to the long-term consequences, even in their teens. That is why they are ours until they are at least 18.

If they do not demonstrate the maturity necessary to handle different aspects of technology appropriately, then they don't deserve to have the technology, for both their safety and the safety of others. Don't be afraid to be the bad guy, since you know your child better than anyone and it is your job to be their parent, not their friend.

"If we do not teach our children, society will. And they – and we – will live with the results."

– Stephen Covey

TV and Other Tech –
Limits and Age-Appropriateness

Free time with kids. If only it was as ideal in reality as it is in our imaginations (or other people's Facebook posts). Most of us probably get plenty of family together time and have kids who are just the right combination of active, entertained, and bored. When this is the case, there is no reason parents should suffer soul-crushing guilt about letting children watch TV or have other types of screen time.

Even the American Academy of Pediatrics (AAP) has come to recognize the reality of the digital age and its effect on parenting and children. For years, the organization stated that children under 2 should not have any screen time, and that older kids should have no more than two hours, but revised its guidelines in 2016.

Screen Time Recommendations by Age

Little to no screen time for children 0-15 months is still the recommendation, but calling Grandma and Grandpa on FaceTime got the green light. Whether or not grandparents contributed to the organization in order to influence this finding is still under investigation.

But we can all probably agree that in today's world, where families often live thousands of miles apart, giving kids the chance to get to know their grandparents and other family members is a good thing even if a screen is involved.

Starting at 15 months, evidence supports the idea that as long as parents are watching quality educational programming with their kids, it can potentially have a positive impact on language development.

For preschoolers, the studies are even more compelling, suggesting that shows like "Sesame Street" or other high-quality children's programming, such as the kind found on PBS, can help establish early math, literacy, and even social skills. Yet again, parental oversight and involvement are encouraged.

If you are using apps with this age group, parents should try them out themselves first and make sure they are age-appropriate. Many may seem to promote educational concepts, but their design may be too simplistic or the other elements of the game too distracting for there to be any real retention. Interaction is really the key when it comes to successfully using apps for this young age group. Look for apps you can actually play with your kids to help reinforce the skills that they teach.

Overall, television viewing and app usage for kids under 5 should be seen as a tool to engage your children in learning and to connect with them in a new and fun way. Being realistic, sometimes it also needs to be a survival tool. There are days that don't go the way we planned, long car rides or plane trips where kids need to be occupied – and honestly, sometimes parents just want to be able to enjoy a meal in peace.

Technology isn't a babysitter and shouldn't be used in that way regularly. But using reasonable guidelines, parents with toddlers and preschoolers can set healthy boundaries and then decide when the occasional bending of the rules is necessary.

When it comes to our older kids, the AAP seems to have moved away from laying down an absolute set screen time limit. There is a growing acknowledgment that technology is pervasive in most kids' lives once they reach school age. Computers are a part of many classrooms, and in some schools, laptops are actually provided for each individual student.

It is not unusual for our kids to spend hours a day on computers at school, as well as at home finishing homework. This academic use alone could easily exceed the standard guidelines that suggest a maximum of two hours per day. This creates stress for parents as we worry about "excessive" screen time. Plus, it can create unwanted battles with our kids, who then want additional screen time for fun.

In today's world, parents need to focus more on balance of activities. There is absolutely evidence that shows the more time an adolescent spends in front of a screen, the more at risk they are for obesity and its related medical issues. In addition, another issue is how technology is interfering with our kids' sleep. This can be the result of exposure to the blue light from today's modern devices, or from staying up later than parents realize, texting friends or playing games, if these devices are allowed to be kept in their rooms at night.

So how do parents find a realistic approach for tweens, teens, and tech? First, it's about making sure you encourage your kids to pursue non-screen-related activities. Considering the emphasis on extracurricular activities today, most kids have an almost endless list of options. Sports, dance, theater, music, Boy Scouts and Girl Scouts – there has to be something your kid can get into that doesn't involve a screen.

At home, it's about setting screen time limits. If you need a little help with this, there are plenty of parental control apps that can help (we talk about specific ones a little later in this book). Using these apps, you can automatically set stop times for certain games and devices, as well as times when the device turns off completely for homework or bedtime.

Also, remember two of the important family tech rules we covered earlier: no tech at the dinner table and no tech behind closed doors.

Overall, as long as you're making sure your child's week is filled with a good variety of activities, don't feel like you have to monitor their tech time usage to the minute. Some days there may be more time playing video games or watching YouTube, but other days they may never even turn on their devices.

Appropriate Content

While HOW MUCH time our kids spend online or watching programming tends to get a tremendous amount of focus, the bigger struggle really comes when we talk about WHAT our kids are viewing.

Everything is great when our children are little, but what happens when they start outgrowing the fun educational apps that are actually teaching them useful skills, or the generally harmless content found on Disney Jr., Nick Jr. and PBS?

It almost seems like we go directly from Paw Patrol and Doc McStuffins to teen drama and dating.

Our 6- or 7-year-olds are still years away from tweendom, but this is the jump that many popular kids games and networks take.

Apps are covered in a later chapter, but let's address the television issues. Many of the characters featured on so called "tween" programming – which targets kids as young as 6 and 7 – don't exhibit the kind of behavior we want to encourage in our children. This is really true no matter what age they are, but definitely not our pre-adolescents. Plus, why are all the parents either absent or idiots?

Let's just leave Max and Ruby out of this so things don't get even more confusing.

It is possible to find age-appropriate shows that kids will find engaging, and that don't push them into territory that we think they aren't ready for – and that we KNOW we definitely aren't ready for.

If you are looking for some viable alternatives, start with your own childhood and try out a few shows that you loved, like "Little House on the Prairie," "Full House," "The Brady Bunch," "Boy Meets World," and others.

You can often find many of these series available at your local library. In fact, the library is a great resource for finding all sorts of kid-appropriate shows and movies totally for free.

Also, as more and more families ditch standard cable in favor of streaming services like Netflix, Hulu and Amazon, a whole new world of quality children's programming is opening up. Many of these services have begun developing their own kids shows that are truly engaging and inventive. They break out of the box of the standard formula that has been around for ages and tap into the imaginations and interests that are specific to newer generations.

Lastly, the world of YouTube has expanded the very definition of children's electronic entertainment. In this world, kids can search on just about any topic that interests them and find a wealth of videos to choose from. There are even dozens of YouTube channels that are just for kids. The only thing to keep in mind with YouTube is that you need to monitor what your children are accessing and make sure the proper restrictions are in place so they aren't viewing material meant for more mature viewers (there is more information on this subject in the YouTube chapter).

As our children get older, we may need to lighten our grip a little bit and allow them to watch some of this more mature programming. There is a certain need for our children to be able to share in the popular culture of their youth to create a sense of fitting in, and that doesn't always have to be a bad thing.

In this situation, we need to take the time to watch some of the shows our kids like with them. It can be a great way to engage and open up conversations on important subjects.

If characters on a certain show are making questionable choices, ask your child what they think about it. Ask them what they might do differently. You can also use this as an opportunity to talk about your own family values and why you may not allow some of the behaviors or activities that children view on TV shows or in movies.

Yes, monitoring how much time our children spend in front of screens, as well as what they are doing and viewing during this time, is a major area of concern for parents today, and it's important. But it doesn't need to be all-consuming.

Setting and following tech rules and using tools, like parental control apps, that are available in abundance can make our lives a whole lot easier. At the end of the day, though, it's really just making sure that we start an ongoing dialogue with our children when they are young and that it continues even as we send them off to college. This allows us to shape their attitudes and interactions when it comes to technology, and to help them learn to make good choices even when we aren't there to watch over them.

Talking With Young Kids About Technology (The Younger Years)

For generations "The Talk" most parents dreaded having with their children was one involving the birds and the bees. However, as technology has taken on a much bigger role in all of our lives, a new awkward conversation has entered the parenting sphere – *"The Tech Talk."*

As parents, we may feel embarrassed about our lack of knowledge about today's technology, or some of the subject matter (like porn), or even that it seems like our kids know more than we do. This could lead us to avoid the topic all together. Unfortunately, our silence puts our children at risk, because ***THE NO. 1 WAY TO KEEP OUR KIDS SAFE ONLINE IS TO TALK WITH THEM.***

While our children may be more comfortable with much of today's technology and understand the mechanics of navigating it better than we do, that doesn't mean that they don't need our supervision and guidance. They may know tech, but **WE KNOW THEM!!!**

We can help our children develop healthy habits and have safe interactions with technology simply by opening up a dialogue that starts when they are toddlers and keeps going well into their teens. All it takes are some simple questions and boundaries at each stage to raise savvy kids who appreciate all of technology's benefits, but also know how to use it safely and responsibly.

Toddler to Preschool

- Establish early on that your children must ask, and receive permission, before using technology devices, and that they must use them with care. See if they know why it's important to turn things off or to put them away where they belong when they're done using them.

- Set time limits, and when it's time to finish ask them to tell you one thing they learned. Follow up with something like, "Technology is fun, because we use our brains, but what aren't we using?" Help them to see the difference between tech time and doing more active things. Believe it or not, this actually will introduce them to the concept of balance and make transitioning to something new easier.

- Spend tech time together each week playing one of their favorite games or reading an interactive story. Ask them questions about what they like or have them tell you their favorite part. Just letting them know you are interested sets a very important foundation for the future.

Early Elementary School

- Many children start taking technology classes as early as kindergarten. Be sure that, when they come home from school, you have them tell you about the material they are covering. What was interesting? What was confusing? Some of the websites they use may be accessible on your home computer, so ask them to show you one of their favorites.

- The school should also send home some kind of parent communication regarding its technology policies. This is a great opportunity to discuss the rules with your child. Ask them, "Why do you think they made these rules? Why is it important to follow them?"

- If you aren't using any child restrictions on your devices at this point, you need to install them. Your children should know those restrictions have been set by you. Explain this to them by asking why some movies are rated "G" and others "PG." Help them to see that, just as some movies are not appropriate for them, some things on the Internet are not okay for them to see or read. Tell them that if they ever see something they think they aren't supposed to online, they should tell you right away, and reassure them they won't be in trouble as long as they are honest with you.

- If your child has begun playing technology-based games with other children (apps, PlayStation, Xbox), start asking them if it is okay to act differently when playing a video game than in other interactions. We know that both children and adults may struggle with being as kind online as they are in real life. This discussion provides your kids with an early introduction to cyber etiquette and the idea that is not okay to treat people differently in one space vs. another.

Later Elementary School

- By the end of elementary school, many kids have cell phones and access to social media. This is when to start talking with your kids about privacy issues. Ask if they know you are supposed to be 13 years old to use most social networks. Inform them that the main reason is because these networks collect personal information about their users.

- Have your kids tell you why it might be important for information about them (like where they live, how old they are, what school they go to) to be kept private. Also, don't forget the ethics of this situation either. Ask them if they think it is okay to lie about your age or join these networks.

- As your child is getting older, they will begin to have broader access to the Internet. This could be at the homes of friends who have less parental supervision or via their own or a friend's mobile phone. You may also have a child who enjoys gaming apps, which sometimes have options to "connect" and play with others they don't know. While I'm sure you probably had the "stranger danger" talk with your kids a long time ago, now you'll want to have the same conversation about strangers online.

Additional tech talk conversation starters for this age group are provided on the resources webpage for this book, found at the end of the book.

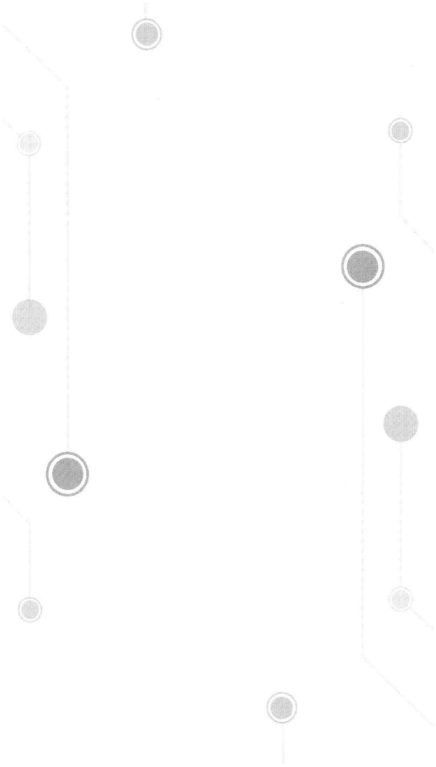

Talking With
Tweens and Teens
About Technology

The technology discussion gets more difficult as our children get older. Touchier subjects come into play and we have less direct supervision of our children as they become more independent. However, these reasons make our involvement even more crucial.

We can't shy away from tackling the tough issues, setting clear rules, and enforcing strict consequences when they aren't followed. The stakes are higher now, both in terms of our children's safety and their futures. One bad decision, such as sharing an inappropriate picture, can follow them in cyberspace for the rest of their lives.

Tweens

Social Media

Social networks either require or strongly suggest that users should be 13 or older before signing up. However, this won't keep a large number of tweens from being active on social media anyway. Ask your child if any of their friends are on Facebook or Instagram. Find out what kinds of things their friends are sharing on these networks. Then ask your child what they think is or isn't okay to share.

Now (yes, now!) is when you must begin to broach the topic of using sexual language or posting sexual pictures online or via text and the potential damage it can cause, both in the short- and long-term. If you need to, give examples of young celebrities they might be aware of who have suffered the damage of such choices.

Apps

If your child has a phone, you also need to be aware of what apps they are using. Many apps can be used by sexual predators to seek out potential victims. For this reason alone, any app on your child's phone should be pre-approved by you. All phones come with the ability to set restrictions that will only allow downloading with a password. You should be the gatekeeper of that password. If you are unsure about any app, Google it – you'll find out quickly whether it's good or bad. (You'll also find more about good and bad apps for kids on our resources webpage, provided at the end of the book.)

Cyberbullying

One of the most unfortunate aspects of today's technology is that it gives many people a false sense of anonymity. As this age group is already prone to a certain amount of teasing and ostracizing, cyberbullying has become a disturbing trend. In worst-case scenarios, it has resulted in some children choosing to take their own lives.

Keep an open dialogue going with your child on this subject and be sure to inquire if they've seen other children treated unkindly. How did this make them feel? How would they feel if it was them? Also, while it is normal for tweens to be moody and somewhat withdrawn, be watchful for dramatic or unhealthy behavior changes, as they could be an indication that your child is being bullied. (More information is provided in the chapter dedicated to this topic later in the book.)

Teens

Social Media

At this point, children are old enough to legitimately open social media accounts. While some parents may still be tempted to forbid their teens from being on social media, you're going to have to let go on this one, at least gradually. Teens need to learn to navigate this tech terrain, and they will require your oversight to help them become responsible social media users. They are also going to need your support in managing the ways social media can affect their self-esteem.

Start with one social media platform and monitor their interactions. Remind them that most people only put their best selves forward on social media and so they should be careful about comparing themselves to what they see. Also, if it really poses a problem, help them evaluate whether or not they are really suited to certain types of social media. It can be helpful to share any of your own struggles on these fronts as well, so they see that it is a problem even for adults.

Digital Citizenship

If you've had technology talks with them starting early, the foundation for this should be well established. However, it is still important to reinforce the importance of being kind and respectful online. At this age too, you need to make sure that your children know that if they see something going on online that makes them uncomfortable or that they feel is morally wrong, they need to come to you. Tell them that they are growing up and you are proud of them, but that sometimes they still need the adults in their lives to help them out – and that's okay.

Planning for the Future

Teens, by nature, live very much in the moment, and it is hard for them to think about how their actions today could impact them five or ten years in the future. However, as they get ready to go to college and to pursue a career, they face a risk that didn't exist for earlier generations: They have an online footprint that is almost impossible to erase.

ges, prospective employers and even, some day, their own children will be able to access their entire digital history, both written and in images. Ask them if anything you've ever posted has embarrassed them. Have them imagine themselves in an interview for a job and being asked about something they posted online. The less you make it a lecture and the more you provide relatable examples for them, the better they will be able to process the long-term consequences of their teen tech choices.

Additional tech talk conversation starters for this age group are provided on the resources webpage for this book, found at the end of the book.

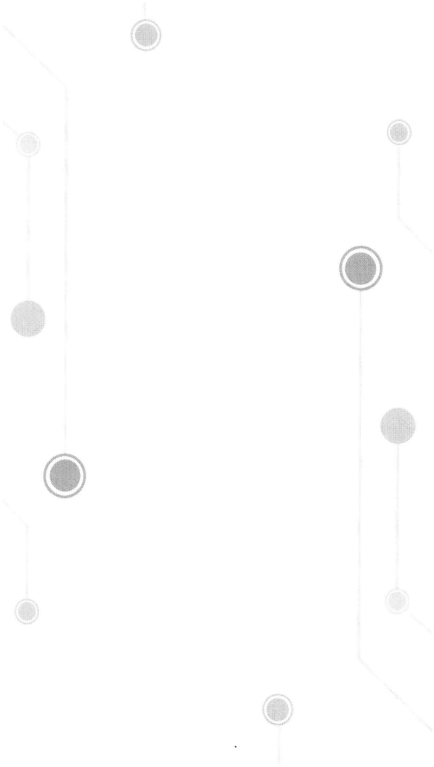

Social Media

Technology is a part of our culture and our families that is here to stay, and that isn't necessarily bad. When we set guidelines and boundaries within our families, as outlined in our Family Tech Rules chapter, technology can have a lot of benefits.

Yet, when we talk about technology, it goes beyond TV watching and video games. We must also consider social media for kids. Social media has proven to be an amazing resource for good in our world. We've seen social media unite and rally people around a cause or need like nothing else. However, we also know there are many negatives to social media for kids, including cases of bullying, inappropriate content and pictures, and child predators.

Most of us have a variety of social media accounts and we enjoy them for various reasons, but even adults can struggle with some of the challenges social media presents. Moms, especially, can find themselves playing the comparison game and feeling bad about themselves when their life doesn't look "Pinterest perfect." Knowing how social media can undermine the confidence of many adults is reason enough to be hesitant and cautious about giving young kids access to social media.

Social Media for Kids: Recommendations and Laws

Honestly, social media really shouldn't be a part of any child's life before the age of 13, no matter what. Not only is it NOT recommended for children under that age to have social media accounts, it is also in violation of many of the social sites' policies. In some cases, it could even technically be considered breaking the law according to the Children's Online Privacy Protection Act, also known as COPPA.

Facebook's terms and conditions actually state, *"You will not use Facebook if you are under 13."* Despite this fact, more than 38% of kids on Facebook are under the age of 13. When a child creates a Facebook profile, they have to attest to the fact that they're at least 13 years of age. So, if you have a child under the age of 13 who you have knowingly allowed to have a FB account, what you're saying to your kid is that rules, and even laws, don't matter. In your mind, maybe using Facebook when they are underage is just a little thing. It's not like you're giving them alcohol or helping them cheat on schoolwork, right?

Either we follow the rules or we don't. Kids lack the ability to discern which are big rules and which are small ones, and overall, we're sending them the message that the rules don't apply to them. If we're concerned about an entitlement generation, here is where it starts.

Oh, and while we are on the subject, let's talk age limits for other social media. These have been taken directly from the terms of use for each of these social media sites:

SNAPCHAT: "No one under 13 is allowed to create an account or use the Services."

PINTEREST: "Any use or access by anyone under the age of 13 is prohibited."

INSTAGRAM: "You must be at least 13 years old to use the Service."

TWITTER: Twitter removed the directly stated age limit from its terms of service several years ago, but does say the following in its privacy policy: "Our Services are not directed to persons under 13." and "We do not knowingly collect personal information from children under 13."

YOUTUBE: "In order to create a YouTube account, we require users to confirm that they are at least 13 yrs. old. Users who enter any age younger than 13 will be prohibited from creating YouTube accounts."

Why Saying "NO" to Social Media for Kids Under 13 is the Right Choice

Let's say your tween daughter really wants a Pinterest account. It may seem like the most harmless of the social media offerings, and you maybe even consider it. Unfortunately, if you take some time to really evaluate the potential issues, you may be less inclined to open an account for her.

Even if you're not intentionally looking for adult material on sites like Pinterest or Instagram, a lot of inappropriate images can appear in the user's home feed. Plus, Pinterest allows advertising, which means there is even less monitoring of what content appears now and your child can be directly targeted for marketing messages that may play into her normal adolescent insecurities.

This story may better capture the concerns around social media and younger kids:

One mom has a 12-year-old daughter who she agreed could get a Pinterest account. Over time, as the mom observed her daughter's usage, she began to notice that her daughter would pin things and then check to see how many "likes" her pins received, or if her friends were repinning them. When there was little or no response, she would pin new things and again wait to see what others thought of them.

She would become visibly upset when her pins received less likes or interaction than someone else's. Overall, this girl took a platform meant for exploring one's interests and turned it into a popularity contest that either provided validation or rejection of her personally.

Before you label this a problem unique to this girl, let's remember this girl is 12. Do you remember twelve? Twelve is middle school, a three-year trial of insecurity, acne, self-doubt, rejection, hormones, emotions, and raw feelings. Everyone experiences self-esteem issues, from the popular kids to the ones who just blend in with the crowd. This mother saw her daughter struggling with herself, questioning her value in a new way, and decided that Pinterest wasn't something she was ready for. Her daughter agreed with little complaint.

These early teen years are hard enough to navigate, as parents. Why should we allow yet another platform for insecurity and doubt?

Saying "no" to social media prior to high school doesn't make you a helicopter parent. Our younger children deal with plenty of teasing, social rejection, and natural life lessons in their real lives, which we are powerless to protect them from. When we do have the ability to avoid or remove an influence that most of our children don't have the maturity or self-confidence to manage in a healthy and safe way, then we are loving them, not sheltering them.

They'll have plenty of time to face the challenges of social media when they get to high school. Childhood is short enough these days — there's no need to hurry it along when we don't have to.

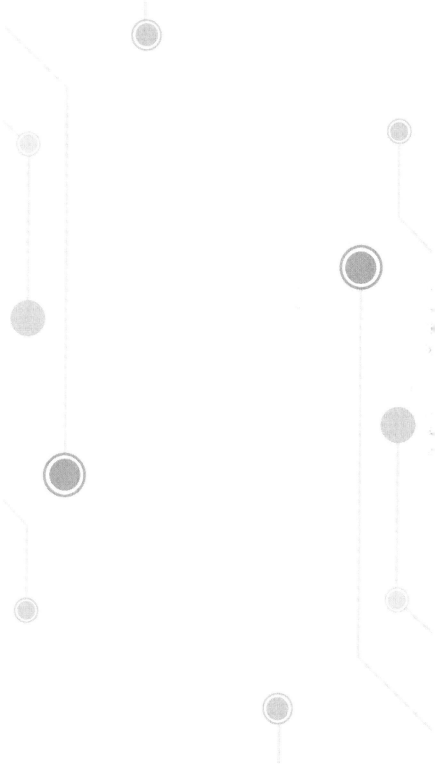

What You Need to Know About YouTube

Yes, this one earned its own chapter. Our children have embraced this video-based social media website with enthusiasm. Unlike Facebook or Snapchat, which really are purely social in nature and intended for more mature users, YouTube actually has both educational and entertainment value for younger kids.

Silly pet tricks, laughing babies and MINECRAFT tutorials are just a few of the things our kids LOVE to watch on YouTube. It can absolutely be a fun experience for our kids (and us too!), as well as a place for them to gain some amazing knowledge.

Here are just a few ways you can use YouTube in your family:

1.   Ideas for new and more complex Lego creations

2.   Instructional videos for projects (This was HUGE for rainbow looms)

3.   Insider tips for their favorite games (Fortnite, Minecraft, Pokemon, Harry Potter, you name it)

4. Supplemental Academic Resources (phonics, science experiments, math concept tutorials)

While there are tons of great resources on YouTube, it is still a website that has limited filtering of its content. As parents, we have to be aware of what our kids are searching for and watching, because filtering content is a little trickier on this platform.

Simple searches that may seem innocent enough can turn up results that are anything but age-appropriate. In addition, some people – both intentionally and unintentionally – include inappropriate language and images in videos aimed at children, and it isn't always immediately evident. Luckily, there are several tools and tips for parents that can make YouTube a safer environment for our kids.

SAFETY FILTERS BY DEVICE

First, there is a simple setting that can be found if you scroll to the bottom of YouTube's main page when using a desktop computer. Here you'll find a little box labeled "SAFETY." You want to switch that to the "ON" position.

Since more and more kids are using YouTube on mobile devices or iPads, for those devices you'll have to take a few different steps:

If your child is using a browser and not an APP to access YouTube:

On the YouTube mobile site:

1. In the upper left of the screen, you will see an arrow in a red box with "YouTube" directly after it – click the arrow.

2. A menu you will pop up with an image of a small gear in the upper right – click the gear.

3. You will now be at a MENU with SETTINGS as the first option. Just below will be an option for "SAFETY MODE" – switch it from "OFF" to "ON" (just touch the word "off" and it will change it to "on").

If your child is using an APP on an iPhone, iPad, or Android Phone, Safety Mode is NOT Available. However, you can – and should – set up Safe Search.

On an Android:

1. Go to MENU, then to SETTINGS, then to SEARCH, then to SAFE SEARCH FILTERING.

2.   Change the SAFE SEARCH FILTER to "Strict" (there is moderate option, but, especially for younger kids, "Strict" is optimal.

On and iPhone or iPad:

1.   In the top left corner are three bars (this is the menu) – tap the bars.

2.   A menu will open with a picture of a gear in the top right corner – tap the gear.

3.   The very first options will be "Safe Search Filtering" and then the words "Don't Filter" to the right.

4.   Tap "Don't Filter" and then change the setting to "Strict."

Watch it With Them or Watch it First

I wish keeping our kids safe from unwanted content on YouTube was as easy as flipping on those safety filters. Unfortunately, while it definitely will eliminate many of the potential hazards for children, it's not perfect. Even YouTube's own disclaimer states: "No filter is 100% accurate." At the end of the day, it still is going to be better if you watch videos on YouTube with your kids or pre-screen them before they watch.

Over time, as you and they become more familiar with YouTube, you'll begin to identify certain individuals and channels that you can rely on to be kid-friendly. At that point, to give them and you a little more freedom, you can consider setting up subscriptions on YouTube for favorites. This will allow your children to go directly to the pre-approved content in the future, rather than having to search.

Getting Started with Kid-Friendly YouTube Videos

If you're looking for a few places that are well-regarded and where you can be confident you'll find quality content for kids on YouTube, these channels are worth a look:

Preschool and Early Elementary:

The Learning Station – Singing, dancing, and imagination games will get kids up and moving and having fun.

HooplaKidz – One of the most popular YouTube channels for the pre-school set. Nursery rhymes and other learning fun.

Disney Animation Studios – All the latest and greatest going on in the land of Disney animation.

Sesame Street – Bert, Ernie, Big Bird, and even Oscar

the Grouch will all be happy to welcome you to their neighborhood.

Lego – The title says it all. Everything and anything you might want to know about your favorite building blocks.

Later Elementary, Tween, and Teen:

Steve Spangler's Sick Science – Move over Bill Nye, there is a new science guy in town. He's dubbed the "high school science teacher we all wished we would have had." Science made fun for all ages.

Kahn Academy – YouTube is just one of the ways this non-profit is working towards its mission to provide a free education to anyone who wants it around the world. Lessons on almost any subject you and your child can imagine.

National Geographic for Kids – From cute to creepy animals of all kinds, dinosaurs to space travel and science experiments galore, this site is filled with worldly wonders that will captivate kids no matter what they're into.

Ted Talks for Youth – Many adults are familiar with Ted Talks, but may not know about this series given by kids on many fascinating topics. A good option for tweens and teens.

What You Need to Know
About Apps

As parents today, everywhere we look it seems there are kids of all ages using and playing on apps on their phones or their parents' phones.

Considering all the apps that are out there targeted towards kids, it can be hard to sort the good from the bad, and even harder to understand how best to monitor and manage our kids' usage of them.

But apps are quickly becoming an integrated part of our children's lives. Many kids no longer watch regular programming on TV, but instead use apps like PBS or Netflix to stream their favorite shows whenever and wherever they want. Xboxes and Wiis are collecting dust, as popular gaming apps take over more and more of the gaming space.

And apps aren't just about entertainment for this generation. There are schools using apps for kids to track their homework and grades. Many sports teams are using them for scheduling and general communication. Basically, pretty much anything we can think of that happens in our kids' lives, there's an app for that.

How to Get the 411 on Apps

Does it feel like almost daily, you hear "Hey, Mom or Dad, can I download this new xyz app? Everyone has it!"

While our kids seem to think that the universal endorsement for anything is "everyone has it," parents know all too well that "everyone" can mean anything from literally everyone to one random kid who we've never met.

When we need to know a little bit more about an app before we allow it, the first place to start is in the App Store if you or your child has an iPhone or on Google Play for Android.

All apps have ratings, found in the "information" section of the apps sales page. Here you'll find not only the age guidelines for the app, but also what content might be questionable.

There is also a description section of the app, but some are more useful than others. Many will outline the specific features of the app and indicate if there are in-app purchases. You should also be able to tell from information in the description if the app is single-player or multi-player. Multi-player often means that strangers will be able to connect to play with your child and may be able to interact via a chat function within the game.

Lastly, in a perfect world, parents would also check out the privacy policy for the app. However, be warned, this usually will direct you to the app maker's website, where you'll encounter a rather lengthy document filled with tons of techno jargon. If you find this overwhelming, then a better option would be to do a little follow-up research with Common Sense Media.

Common Sense Media has a website that provides current reviews for parents about the most popular apps. Its age ratings may not always coincide with the information provided by the App Store or Google Play, and parents may find these ratings more accurate and reliable. Additionally, they'll provide more user-friendly warnings about safety and privacy concerns.

There is also a section for parental reviews, which can be quite handy. Other parents are a great source of insider tips and advice. Just be sure to read a good sampling of reviews to get a balanced viewpoint.

Apps: The Good

Staying up to date on apps and managing our kids' usage of them can be a lot to take on, but we shouldn't overlook all the ways that apps can positively contribute to our lives.

Apps really can make some of the more complicated parts of our life easier. Think about online calendars and how they enable us to track the different schedules of all members or our family with color coding and reminders. There are homework apps that can help our kids with everything from figuring out tough math problems to taking notes and organizing their assignments.

If you're a mom of littles, there are even apps that can help you find clean public restrooms with changing tables – whether you're out shopping or on a long road trip to visit Grandma.

One area in particular where apps can truly make a significant difference is for kids with special needs. Apps in no way can take the place of the therapies and other medically endorsed treatments for conditions such as ADHD, autism, dyslexia, dysgraphia, and sensory processing disorders. But they can still be a powerful complementary tool for parents to use at home.

There are dozens of quality apps available that target specific learning challenges. Some can be pricey, but many don't cost more than a cup of coffee, or in some cases are absolutely FREE. Parents can easily find apps to help with a variety of issues, such as communication, language development, executive functioning, managing emotions, auditory processing, and so much more.

Plus, kids today love using technology! Using apps can be an engaging way to get kids with unique struggles to engage in the learning process and help move their progress forward.

The National Association for Child Development is an excellent resource for finding apps that address a range of learning challenges. Additionally, Sunshine and Hurricanes has an extensive library of posts that provide links to some of the best apps we've found, which is available on the resources webpage page for this book, provided at the end of the book.

Minecraft

Yes, this app is getting it's own section because it remains one of, if not the, most popular apps for younger kids to use. My daughter first started using Minecraft on an old iPhone of mine when she was 4. You read that correctly, 4.

Minecraft may seem a little odd with its retro graphics and somewhat addictive appeal. However, it has more of an upside than people realize. Minecraft is not a mindless activity, nor is it like any other gaming app. Players are required to think, create and strategize. It also teaches some pretty high-level engineering concepts, because of the need for spatial understanding (geometry) and design.

The most common version of the game that younger kids play is the pocket edition app, which is available for all types of mobile phones and tablets. But it is important to know that the game is also available for gaming systems like the Xbox and PlayStation, and even for your PC.

The easiest way to describe Minecraft is virtual Legos, but that is definitely an oversimplification. At first the game may appear poorly made or terribly outdated, like some kind of strange old-school video game. However, once you watch your kids in action and see all the ways they use their creativity to construct buildings and interact with their environment, you're likely to recognize the genius of this game's simplicity. In many ways, it's almost a blank canvas without the typical rules and boundaries of a highly designed game. This sense of freedom is a big part of the game's appeal to kids.

Minecraft can be played in two modes: Creative and Survival. Creative is the better option for younger children, end of story. In this mode, players all become the generic character "Steve"(they can add their own name if they prefer, but everyone looks the same) and they are deposited into a Minecraft world that basically looks like a typical landscape, with grass, hills, trees, sky, and some lakes or ponds. There is also the occasional farm animal, such as a sheep.

Players are able to select from a large variety of materials to build any structure they can dream up. They can make houses of stone or glass that can be on the ground or in the air, with gardens and trap doors. Again, it sounds pretty straightforward, but I was amazed when I saw how elaborate and unique my kids' projects were.

Those who have at least a little familiarity with Minecraft are probably wondering about the zombies and the creepers you've heard about. Those appear in the Survival version of the game. Again, due to the rudimentary graphics, these are not super-scary and there is no real blood or gore.

Survivor mode is just like it sounds. In this version of the game, you don't have unlimited access to all the building materials and other resources that are available like you do in the Creative version. You actually have to go out and find them. You start the game during "daytime" and have a limited amount of time to find what you need to stay alive and build some kind of dwelling to keep you safe at night.

Once night falls, all the more sinister elements of Minecraft come out, and you have to fight to survive. Again, this sounds a little bit scary, and you'll have to make the call on the right age for your child to be allowed to switch to this mode of play.

Players in Survivor mode have to be clever and strategize to survive. While you can "die," you basically are just recycled right back into the game again. In either mode, there is no "winning" and no end goal. It is open-ended and just an endless invitation to think bigger and better and create more.

Multi-Player:

The aspect of the game that most kids really enjoy is the fact that they can "connect" with others and play together. But this is often the part that scares parents the most. Now, the word "connect" in the Minecraft sense doesn't mean they are plugging into the whole Internet, where any crazy can hop in their Minecraft world with them. The primary way to "connect" is on a shared network, most commonly your home network, where family members can play with each other or friends who might be over visiting.

Parents should take advantage of the multi-player part of the game and actually play WITH their children so they understand how the basics of the game work. This

this book, that will always have updated info on all the current "hot" gaming apps to help you stay on top of the trends.

Apps – The Not So Good

Okay, for as many ways as apps can help our children, there are plenty of ways that they open them up to harm. The good news is that parents have more control than they think, and there are some fairly simple steps you can take to minimize the risks of using apps.

When children are younger, most of the time if they are using apps it's on a family iPad or on their parents' phones. In both cases, setting up basic parental controls and password protection is key to keeping them (and your bank account) safe. As long as you've set up these devices to ask for a password in order to download an app or make in-app purchases, you've won the biggest battle.

As previously mentioned, when a child is interested in a new app, take a few minutes to read the information page for the app to see the recommended minimum age for users. Also, take a look at what Common Sense Media has to say about the app. Doing those two things before you download should quickly help you to determine if an app is appropriate or not.

Also, keep in mind that, when kids are in elementary or middle school, it is best to steer them clear of most social apps. Almost all of these apps clearly state they are not recommended for kids under 13. The primary reason for this is that social apps are "social," and therefore have some kind of open-access platform that allows users to interact with each other.

Now, that said, there are still some social apps that have become quite popular for younger kids, such as Music.ly and Snapchat. Just because lots of kids are using them doesn't make them safe or smart choices for children. So, be clear about what you are allowing if you're going to let younger children access these apps.

Read the app's (or service's) privacy policy so you understand what information is being shared about your child. Additionally, review the privacy settings, because most of these apps default sharing to "public." Before you allow your child to use any app, re-configure the settings so your child's account is private or can only interact with "friends."

Even when these precautions have been taken, it is best if younger children use these apps with parental supervision. There are still plenty of workarounds and other issues these apps can present.

As kids move into the tween and teen years, social apps are almost inevitably part of their lives. Since these platforms are commonplace, it makes sense to let your children begin using them while they are still under your roof and you have the ability to help them use these apps safely and responsibly.

In general, most teens are not going to get into too much trouble using apps. We need to be careful about allowing our fears in this area to become overinflated. That said, we still need to be smart and involved parents.

It can't be emphasized enough that the single most effective tool we have as parents when it comes to apps and other technology is a conversation. Check in with your kids, talk with them frequently about what's going on in their online world and monitor which apps they are downloading and how they are using them.

Be sure your teens understand that many apps, such as the popular Snapchat, have privacy statements that explain that pictures, videos and other information shared in apps is not necessarily private. Many apps establish the company's ownership of content exchanged in an app, and then there is also a risk of hacking.

Apps – The Bad

There are two types of apps parents should be on the lookout for, especially with teen users. The first kind of app that are a red flag are apps that can be used to hide texts, photos, and videos. These are often referred to as "vault" apps. They change often, so it's difficult to provide a list, but here's what to look out for: These apps usually disguise themselves as an everyday app on your child's phone, something like a calculator. However, when you tap on them, instead of the app automatically opening, it will offer a login screen. Since there is no reason you should need to login to an app like a calculator, that is a giveaway that the app isn't as innocent as it appears.

The second type of app that parents want to keep an eye out for are less-common social apps that, instead of connecting kids to people they know, open them up to strangers. Many of these are actually dating apps or apps meant to be used for exchanging content of a sexual nature. A few well-known apps in this category include Tinder, Kik Messenger, and Omegle. In this area as well, new apps are constantly being developed and gaining in popularity, and the trends come and go as quickly as teen fashion fads.

Overall, trust your gut, and if you're not sure about an app your child wants, that's what Google is for. In a matter of minutes, you should have no problem finding out everything you need to know about an app and whether it's questionable or not.

Also, you will find a more extensive list of both "bad" and "good" apps on the resources webpage for this book, referenced at the end of the book. We attempt to keep the information as updated as possible for parents.

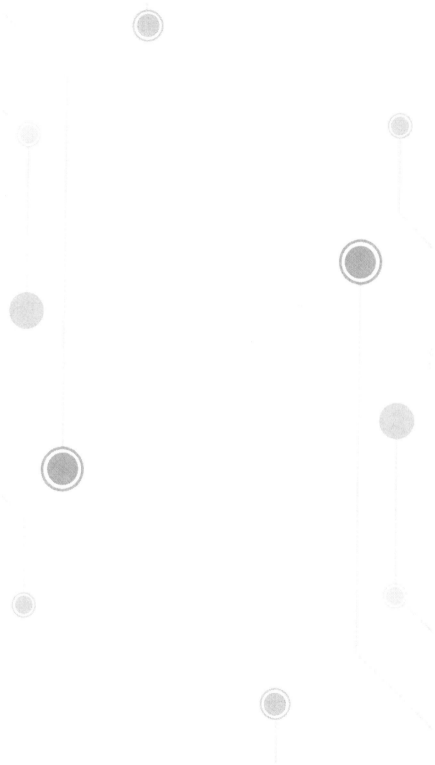

Kids and Mobile Phones

The question is not if, BUT WHEN your child is going to be ready for their very own phone. It is an inevitable right of passage for young people today. But smart parents don't allow outside influences to determine the right time for their child to be given this privilege.

Some parents rush into the decision before their children really are ready. Others wait out of fear, without considering that perhaps their child does have the maturity to handle the responsibility.

What Age is the Right Age?

If you want an exact age, there isn't one. There are many factors to consider. However, while there are some exceptions due to unique family situations, giving a child a cell phone prior to sixth grade doesn't seem necessary or wise.

Don't be afraid to swim against the current when it comes to "trends" that are moving towards giving kids mobile phones earlier and earlier. Many parents will say the main reason they gave their child a phone, some as young as kindergarten, was for safety purposes. The phone makes them feel secure, because it enables them to stay in constant communication with their child and track the child's location.

Unfortunately, what may be happening is that the phone creates a false sense of security. While we think knowing where they are at all times may enable us to protect our children from predators, it can actually open up more avenues for predators to gain access to them. And those who might want to kidnap or otherwise harm a child are going to be smart enough to ditch the cell phone ASAP.

Also, once we give them a phone, we may feel that takes the place of having to educate our children about personal safety. Teaching our kids to check in with us from an early age and to let us know where they are going and with whom develops an important habit. If they haven't been accountable for this starting at a young age, it will be more difficult to enforce this rule as they get older and it becomes even more important.

Things to Consider

Now, there is a point, usually sometime in middle school, when giving a child a cell phone has advantages. As they become more active in school and extracurricular activities or are doing more with friends, being able to coordinate pickups or communicate schedule changes is important. They also need to learn all the lessons that come with cell phone use. This starts with learning accountability and showing they can keep track of the phone and keep it in working order.

Then comes understanding how to communicate intelligently and appropriately, both by phone and text. Many of us might be surprised to discover that our children really don't know how to have a mature phone or text conversation, in which they actually pass along information in a coherent way.

Lastly, we need to begin the progressive education about using a mobile phone safely and what is and isn't okay to send – whether in words or pictures – using the phone's various features, apps and Internet access.

How to Know if Your Child is Ready

So, taking that all into consideration, how do you know if your child is ready for a cell phone? Here's a list of questions that will help you determine if now is the time:

- Is your child responsible at home? Do they complete their chores without being reminded? Is their room in a satisfactory state a majority of the time? Do they care for the toys/technology/clothes they've been given?

- Has your child demonstrated appropriate behavior with other technology at home? Are they following the rules for computer time and video game usage? Do they return games and controllers to the right place, not strewn about on the floor? Do they turn off the TV, games, etc. without arguing?

- Are they giving their best effort in school? Are they respectful at home?

- Do they typically make good decisions even when not being watched?

- Do they understand a cell phone is a privilege, not a right?

- Do they accept responsibility when they make poor choices, rather than blame others?

There is no magic age when a child is ready for a cell phone. But, if you can comfortably answer "yes" to the questions above, it may be time. If in doubt, err on the side of caution and reevaluate in a few months.

Once you've determined your child is mature enough to handle the responsibility that comes with cell phone ownership, then it's time to set some cell phone rules for tweens and teens.

Would You Give Your New Driver a Ferrari?

There are a variety of options for phones these days, so take your time to learn about as many of them as possible before choosing the phone and plan. Think about it this way: Would you give your 16-year-old, brand-new, driver a Ferrari when they receive their license? Probably not. Why? That car has too many bells and whistles and far too much power for a highly under-experienced driver, not to mention its price tag. It would be better to provide a less glamorous, but safe and steady, vehicle – at a more reasonable price point.

Giving your child the latest, greatest, most expensive phone on the market is like giving them a Ferrari, and your child is most likely not ready for all the features it offers, nor have they shown they deserve this level of privilege.

It's wiser to give them an older, reliable phone that is safe and gets the job done. This approach provides your child with the opportunity to show that they can take care of a less expensive phone first and follow the cell phone rules you set for them. Over time, they can earn their way to a more updated phone – or better yet, save their own money to pay for it.

To Surf the Web or to Not Surf the Web?

You'll also need to decide whether you want your child to have Internet access available from their phone. If you are giving a phone to a child in middle school, Internet access isn't advisable. There are too many temptations for an age group that is already struggling with difficult physical and emotional changes.

Start by providing a phone with the internet browser disabled – the privilege of even having a phone is enough for them to handle at first. You can easily turn off Internet browsers in the "settings" of both iPhones and Androids.

They will still be able to text and make calls, as well as listen to music and even use some apps. But remember all of these activities still require data usage. Make sure they know their limits and how to check to make sure they aren't going over. Inform them if they go over on data usage, they'll be responsible for the charges.

Additionally, Internet access on the phone is generally not necessary, because children have opportunities to access the Internet for schoolwork on your home computer or even on school computers, where there is more supervision and better controls. Honestly, it also makes your life as a parent easier, because it is one less thing you have to monitor. Give them the opportunity to prove themselves at one level, before moving onto the areas that become more complex for both them and you to manage.

Cell Phone Contract

Once you reach the point that your child will be getting a phone, it is good to also require them to sign an official contract with you. This is the perfect way to ensure your expectations are clearly outlined and what the consequences will be if they're not met. Some of it may seem like common sense, but it is best for everything to be covered so nothing's left to interpretation.

You will find a link to a printable cell phone contract on the resources webpage for this book, found at the end of the book. It is available for you to print and use for free, or you can use it as an example to create your own. Either way, you'll be glad to have this in place.

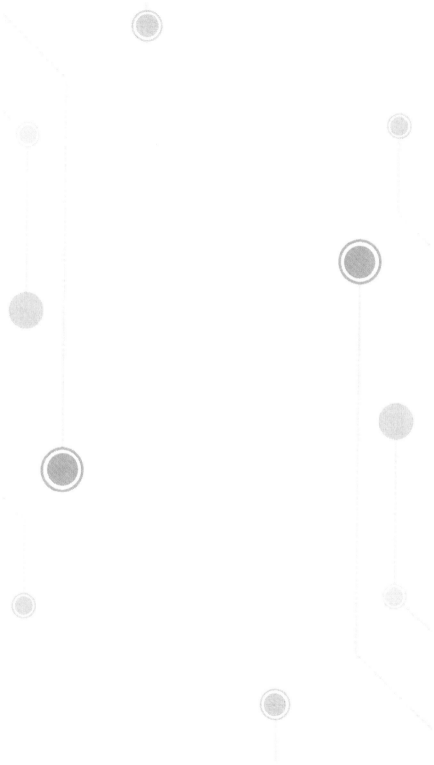

Monitoring Your Child's Phone and Online Activity is NOT Spying

"I trust my child."

"I don't want to invade their privacy."

"My child would NEVER do those things online."

"I'm not going to SPY on my child."

These are often the reasons parents give for not monitoring their kids' online activities. Unfortunately, while the instinct may come from a good place, taking this type of hands-off approach to technology and our kids can be dangerous.

It also raises the question: Why are we so reluctant to monitor our kids online the same way we do offline?

Giving tweens and teens (and in some cases even younger children) complete freedom in the online world is giving them too much autonomy that they aren't ready for yet. It is placing adult privileges and responsibility on their shoulders, but they are not adults. Plus, let's face it: Most of us know plenty of adults who don't handle themselves appropriately online.

Research has shown that the frontal lobe of the human brain doesn't fully develop until sometime in a person's 20s, and this is the part of the brain that governs impulse control and risk-taking behavior. This is why teenagers are notorious for making poor and shortsighted decisions, and why children in general need parental oversight and involvement.

Just one cautionary tale of many from across the nation is a story out of Colorado, where more than HALF the students at one high school were caught participating in a nude photo exchange. Hundreds of photos of a sexual nature were discovered, including photos of children who were as young as eighth graders.

Of course, we all want to think the best of our kids, but understanding and not being naive about their limitations is how we keep our children safe and help them learn to navigate the world around them.

No one questions why we stand beneath our toddler when they try to climb the jungle gym for the first time. It's because we don't know for sure what they are capable of and we need to be there in case they fall. We don't refuse to attend parent/teacher conferences or throw away our children's report cards without looking at them out of fear that our children will think we are invading their privacy.

And as our children get old enough to drive and to go out with friends on their own, we don't require them to tell us where they will be going because we don't trust them. We do it because, as parents, we recognize it is our responsibility to know where our kids are, who they are with, and what they are doing.

Why is it any different when it comes to what they are doing on a computer, mobile phone, or any technological device?

Why do we care who they are hanging out with in real life, but we may have no idea who they are friends with on Facebook or Instagram or Snapchat?

Why would we keep them from watching PG-13 and R-rated movies, because they are too young for them, but we wouldn't investigate the age recommendations for many apps they are using or various forms of social media?

If we are going to be involved parents, who take an interest in our children's lives, this has to include technology. Just think about the amount of time our kids spend using technology today! We can't exclude from our involvement something that consumes almost as much of their time as many of their extracurricular activities.

Also, even the best kids make mistakes. That is part of growing up. Think back to when you were in middle school and high school, and some of the unfortunate choices you made. Now, imagine if some of those stories, or worse yet photos, made their way onto today's social media.

Unfortunately, until recently, most youthful screwups often faded away with the passing of time. Now, one stupid Facebook post or a photo texted to a single person can be passed onto hundreds and even thousands of people in an instant, and can never be deleted from the online identity that will follow our children their entire lives.

Is it unfair that the stakes are SO high for our kids? Absolutely. Are the risks potentially overblown, like so many dangers for our kids these days? Probably. Welcome to the unique challenges of modern parenting.

You can meet those challenges, though, using the tried and true parenting techniques of setting expectations and just staying engaged with your kids and aware of what they are doing.

Parental Controls and Monitoring Options

There are many options available for parents to help us keep track of how much time our kids are spending on different devices and what they are doing during that time.

If we are upfront with our kids that we will be checking their online activity – such as sites they are visiting, what they post online, texts and photos they are taking and sending – then it's not spying. We're not being secretive or sneaky, and we're not invading their privacy.

Some of the more popular monitoring tools for parents include:

- Net Nanny

- Circle with Disney

- My Mobile Watchdog

- Symantec Norton Family Premier

- Qustodio

- Forcefield

- OurPact

Almost all of these products give parents the ability to set up customized profiles for each child. This is important because a 4-year-old is likely to be given far less freedom than a 10-year-old. Within each child's profile, you will be able restrict certain websites and apps, as well as limit time spent on specific apps, on websites, and on the devices as a whole.

Some of these tools also give parents the ability to monitor texts, activity on social networks, and pictures sent to and from the phone. Be sure to do your research when deciding which one is right for your family, links to these various monitoring options are available on the resource webpage for this book, provided at the end of the book.

Technology is a privilege our children enjoy. It is not a right – it is something they earn. Privacy when using technology is the same. As they get older and demonstrate they deserve more freedom, we can give it.

Whether it is their everyday lives or their online lives, the rules should be the same, and our kids need to know we care and will be involved in both equally. We owe them that much. Monitoring our kids online isn't spying – it's simply parenting with a 21st-century twist.

Tweens, Teens, Texting, Sexting, and Acronyms

You may have seen in the media or read articles in your social media feeds about all the different texting acronyms parents should be aware of. However, what many parents don't know is that a large number of texting acronyms are inaccurately defined, and even if that isn't the case, most are already outdated.

So, why do these acronyms keep circulating?

Because, while they aren't successful at properly educating parents, they are FANTASTIC at feeding parents' worst fears about tweens, teens, and texting.

Do you want to know what the real story is when it comes to tweens, teens, and sexting? In reality, most kids are not out there "sexting" on a regular basis. Reported percentages vary, with the high end being 20% and the low end around 7%.

In most cases, the likelihood to engage in "sexting" goes up with age, and the greatest percentages are seen in older teens (17+). However, the definition of "sexting" is also not very clear. It can be anything from exchanging some fairly harmless and vague hormone-fueled texts to the more serious, but far less prevalent, instances of sending sexually graphic texts and photos of a sexual nature.

Texting Acronyms – Be Smart, Not Scared

As parents, we would prefer none of this was going on via text, but we must also understand that part of it is just the modern-day version of the very normal expression of early sexuality. Also, while technology may be providing a new platform for this expression, it isn't contributing to any increase in teen sexual activity.

In fact, depending on the data source, teen sex rates have, at worst, stayed constant during the last 20 years, or have actually declined as much as 7%.

Now, this doesn't mean that parents can sit back and take a head-in-the-sand approach to the whole topic of inappropriate texting acronyms and "sexting." It is still happening, and many tweens and teens who admit to engaging in "sexting" say they did so because of peer pressure.

One of the best defenses parents have to combat the influence of this kind of negative peer pressure is to simply keep an open and honest dialogue going on with their kids. We need to be willing to tackle the tough talks and make sure kids know the risks.

Make Sure Kids Understand the Risks

While our kids may think sexting a photo to their boyfriend or girlfriend is safe, because this other person cares about them, they need to think about what might happen if they break up, and how such photos could then be used to hurt them.

Help them to understand that once a sext is sent, whether it is only text or includes pictures, it can never be completely deleted. There can also be legal consequences to sexting, which in some states is considered child pornography distribution.

Also, if you are genuinely concerned about the possibility of your child sending or receiving inappropriate texts, this is not something that is out of your control. There are numerous ways you can manage this situation with monitoring apps and software that mentioned in chapter 10 and which can be found on the resources webpage for this book, provided at the end of the book.

What Exactly Do Those Texting Acronyms Mean?

Should you come across any acronyms in your child's texts that you are not familiar with, you can look almost any of them up using the Urban Dictionary. This site is a user-generated online dictionary of slang terms and phrases. I'm going to warn you: This isn't a site for the faint-of-heart, but it will give you the information you need to know. However, I bet most parents will be pleasantly surprised when they discover 2G4E simply means "together forever" or WYCM means "will you call me."

Yes, our kids are growing up fast, but maybe not as fast as we are led to believe. If you DBEYR (don't believe everything you read) and practice smart parenting by going ISO (in search of) real facts, these tween and teen years might not be so bad, and could even be GR8 (great)! TTYL. :)

Cyberbullying

Did you know that some estimates say that more than half of all children are likely to experience cyberbullying? In today's world, where technology has become an everyday part of our children's lives, parents must realize bullying has moved beyond its traditional forms and has taken on a whole new life in the online realm.

By the time a child reaches middle school, almost ALL of their classmates will have phones, and many will have access to social media – despite the fact that the earliest recommended age is 13. If you have a child in middle school or older, you've probably already heard stories about other children who have been harassed via text by young people they thought were their friends. Plus, we're all familiar with the tragic incidents covered in the news about teenagers taking their lives after particularly vicious cyberbullying episodes. It breaks a parent's heart!

While we often worry about our kids being the victims of cyberbullying, it's also important to note that the facts show our children may be just as likely to be the ones doing the bullying. In either case, we should all want to do whatever we can to keep children safe and to minimize the impact of this damaging trend on today's young people.

What is cyberbullying exactly?

It comes in many forms, but includes all of the following:

- Sending hurtful messages or threats via email or text, or posting them to social media networks

- Sending or posting inappropriate pictures of another person via text, social networks, or email

- Spreading rumors online or through texts

- Breaking into another person's email or social media accounts to send false messages

Why does bullying occur?

Although commonly associated with poor self-esteem, children with high self-esteem who think they are superior and are entitled to treat others poorly can just as often perpetrate bullying. Bullying is about control, and there is no one profile that fits bullies – they come in all shapes and sizes and can be found across all age groups. Bullying can also result from being bullied or even abused in the home environment.

What can parents do?

Parents who are often very hands-on in every other area of their child's lives may not have the same involvement when it comes to their children's online activities. Many parents do not install any kind of parental controls on their children's devices, they are unaware of the suggested age requirements for children to participate in social media, and they hesitate to monitor their children's online activity because they think of it as spying.

Unfortunately, this lack of supervision is part of what is fueling the increase in cyberbullying. Kids feel they have more freedom and anonymity in the online space, and therefore are emboldened to say and do things they might not in more monitored or less-anonymous environments. Also, because parents aren't asking more questions and talking with their kids about technology, children are less likely to tell their parents what is going on or to seek help if they are experiencing cyberbullying.

As a parent, it may be difficult to know how you can help your child avoid being bullied, especially if you are unfamiliar and uncomfortable with today's technologies and social networks. However, you don't need to be a "techie" to be an informed and responsible parent in this area.

When it comes to bullying, parents have an extremely powerful weapon at their disposal. It's called a *conversation.*

The simple act of talking with children regularly and being involved in their lives (sometimes whether they want us to be or not) can be the key to keeping them safe. Maintain an ongoing dialogue with them about privacy, online etiquette, and what is or isn't appropriate to share or say online. Also, make sure they understand that once they post something online, they can't take it back.

What Tools are Available to Parents?

Because talking with kids has been identified as the No. 1 way to prevent cyberbullying, SAMHSA (the Substance Abuse and Mental Health Services Administration) released the "Know Bullying" app as a resource for parents. The app has conversation starters that parents can use to open up everyday dialogue with their children. There are also tips to prevent bullying by different age groups, warning signs, reminders, and social media strategies. There is even a section for educators, with ideas to prevent bullying in the classroom.

The numerous easy-to-use privacy settings on computers, web browsers, and cell phones can also help protect children. Many are referenced in other chapters in this book, and parents can also find step-by-step instructions on how to use these tools through this book's resources webpage, provided at the end of this book.

Conclusion and Resources

Much of today's parenting overwhelm when it comes to technology is rooted in our perception that it has added a whole new layer of complexity that requires extensive research and time to understand. Plus, because new technology is always coming on the scene, it can feel like it is impossible to keep up, which leaves parents feeling defeated before they even try.

Well, here's the thing. Technology is constantly changing and updating, but smart parenting hasn't changed for generations. It's all about taking proven parenting principles and adapting them to the current challenges. The advice, tips and strategies we provided in this book should help you do just that.

Now this doesn't mean that some work won't be involved, but no one ever said parenting was going to be a cakewalk. The good thing is that the same technology that is causing all the problems also provides many of the solutions.

In many cases, a simple Google search or visit to a few tried and trusted websites can give us the information we need in a matter of minutes. We're making it even easier for you by providing a resource page on our blog. Here you'll find links to all the websites and tools we mention in the book, including the following:

- Tech Rules Printable

- AAP Guidelines

- Best Apps for Kids Link (Ours)

- Monitoring Apps and Parental Controls Software

- Bullying Websites

- Common Sense Media

- Cell Phone Contract

- How to set parental controls by device

To access this page you will need a special password. You're receiving this as a bonus for buying this book, so we hope you won't share it with others.

sunshineandhurricanes.com/
screen-time-sanity-resources
Password: S&HSmartTechParent

No matter what age your children are or how confident you feel or don't feel about all this technology stuff, realizing that you can't bury your head in the sand is the hardest step. All you have to do after that is keep on walking. No one expects us to be perfect parents, we just have to care and be willing to do our best. You got this!

"There is no such thing as a
perfect parent, so just be
a real one."

- Sue Atkins

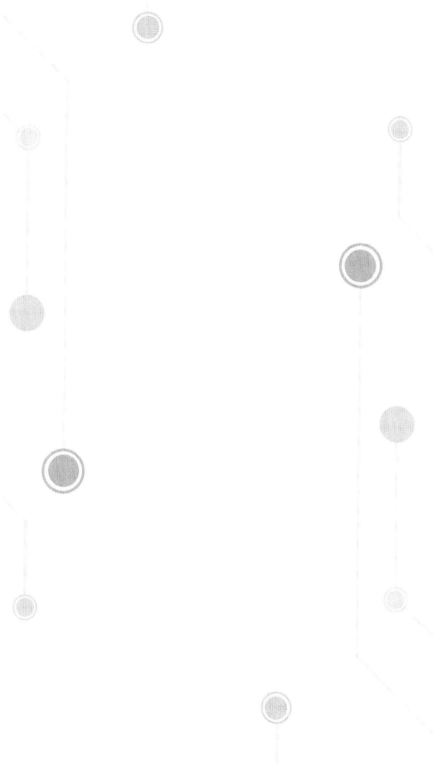

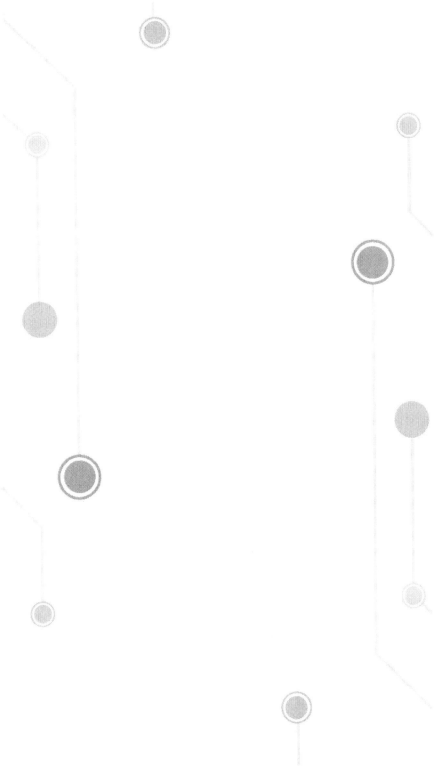

About the Authors

Kira Lewis is currently a free-lance writer and speaker, but in her past life she spent 15 years in corporate marketing. She is a graduate of the University of Michigan (Go Blue!) and has an MBA from Southern Methodist University. She and her husband Phil are raising their two kids, a son (13) and daughter (9) in sunny Florida where they love to boat when they aren't at soccer games or dance practices.

Michelle Myers holds a dual degree in Education and Human Resource Management and is a former teacher and education trainer. She currently works as a Connections Director at New Hope Presbyterian Church in SouthWest Florida. Michelle and her husband Mark have four children, 3 daughters (16, 10, &7) and a son (12) and as if that didn't keep them busy enough, they also are very active in their community and church.

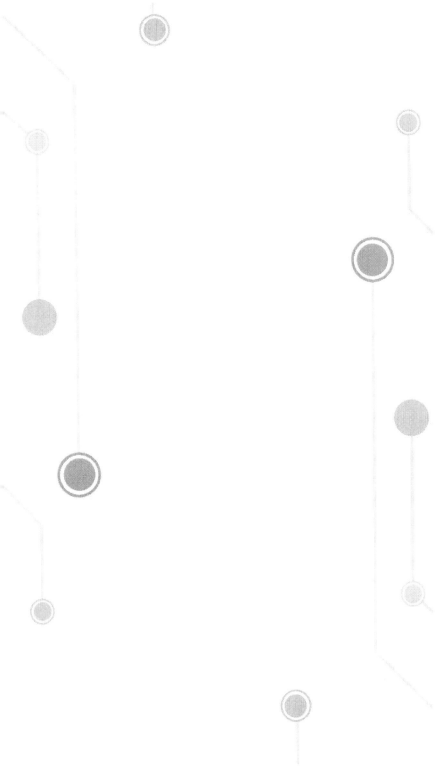

Connect with the Authors

Facebook

facebook.com/SunshineandHurricanes

facebook.com/parentingkidsandtechnology

Pinterest

pinterest.com/sunandhurricane

Instagram

instagram.com/sunandhurricanes

Twitter

twitter.com/sunandhurricane

Email

http://bit.ly/2dtPyvP

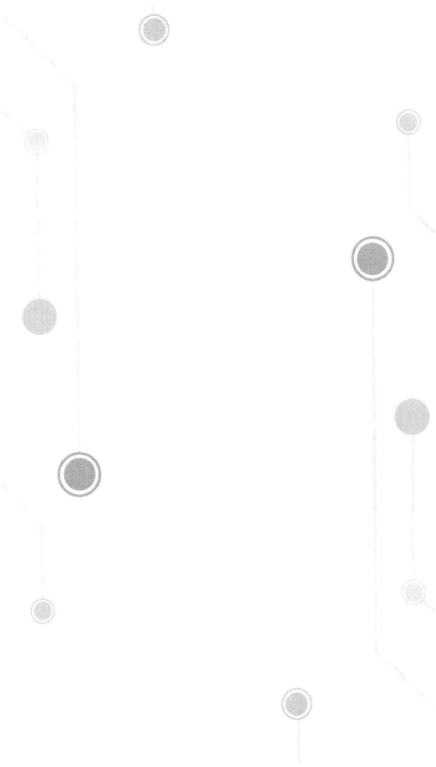

Made in the USA
Lexington, KY
20 April 2018